Slacks
Fitting
Book

Slacks Fitting Book

by Nancy Zieman

Nancy's Notions, Ltd., Beaver Dam, WI

Updated Edition:
Edited by Rebecca Dumlao

Designed by Laure Noe

Illustrations by Rochelle Stibb

Typesetting by Kathleen Hasson & Phyllis Novak

Original Edition:
Artist Janet Asbury

Edited by Nancy E. Brown & Phyllis Novak

Original Edition © 1982 Nancy's Notions, Ltd.

Acknowledgements
Special thanks to Ruth Oblander who taught me the foundations of fitting patterns; The McCall Pattern Co.; my marketing staff of Kathleen Hasson, Phyllis Novak, and Donna Fenske who have provided valuable information for this book; and all the consumers who have shared their fitting concerns and solutions.

Table Of Contents

Letter from Nancy

Fitting slacks isn't my favorite part of sewing, but it's extremely important. After all, it is so uncomfortable to wear an ill-fitting pair of slacks!

Unlike fitting blouse, jacket and dress patterns, there is a specific start-to-finish sequence for fitting a slacks pattern. To simplify this process, I've written the Slacks Fitting Book like a recipe. Follow the "slacks recipe" which includes six, step-by-step "Alteration Units" for the most accurate results.

Make the fitting process fun! Invite a sewing friend to join you; each of you can alter a pair of slacks at the same time. Allow a couple of hours for this fitting process, it takes time to fit slacks. But once you have a pair of slacks that fit, simply use the pattern over and over again.

Sewing is an enjoyable skill and hobby. It is even more pleasurable when working with patterns that fit!

Happy Fitting & Sewing!

Nancy Zieman

About The Author

Nancy Zieman is a busy woman who loves to sew! She is the producer and host of cable and public television's **"Sewing With Nancy"** and President of Nancy's Notions, Ltd., a mail order business of sewing supplies.

Besides authoring **The Slacks Fitting Book**, Nancy has also written **The Busy Woman's Fitting Book** and **The Busy Woman's Sewing Book** with Robbie Fanning. She has a B.S. degree in Home Economics from the University of Wisconsin—Stout.

Fitting - Not Fun But Necessary

Fitting isn't much fun. Most people would rather concentrate on other parts of their sewing. But fitting is necessary. Nobody wants slacks that look sloppy or feel too tight. Getting a pair of slacks to fit perfectly takes some time and effort, but the end results are well worth it!

Introduction to Pivot-Slide Alterations

My experience in sewing seminars and on television indicates that programs on fitting, especially slacks, remain favorites. This book is designed to help you get a good fit in slacks using the pivot and slide method.

You may be familiar with other techniques. *Slashing and spreading, folding and tucking, and "add a dab or take off a pinch"* methods are common and can work, but they can also lead to big mistakes.

Folding and Tucking is often combined with *slashing and spreading*. With both methods, the seam and pattern lines are easily changed, causing the shape to change.

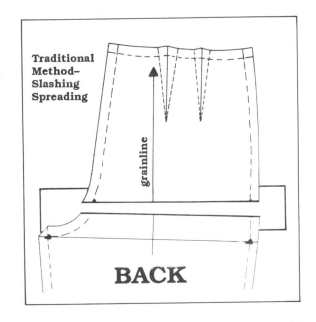

Traditional Method– Slashing Spreading

grainline

BACK

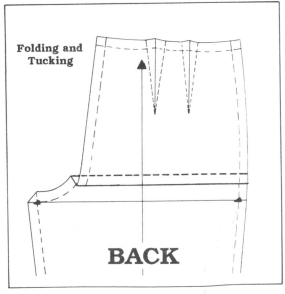

Folding and Tucking

BACK

Add a dab or *take off a pinch* are probably the most common changes made by many of us. Adding or subtracting at the side seams by simply re-drawing the cutting lines, causes a miss-match of seams and the grainline to "tip."

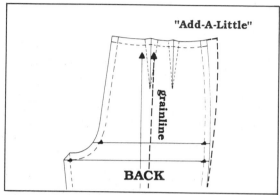

Pivot-Slide Alterations are a newer approach to fitting. The advantage of using these techniques is that the alterations are added or subtracted evenly on both sides of the grainline and the cutting lines.

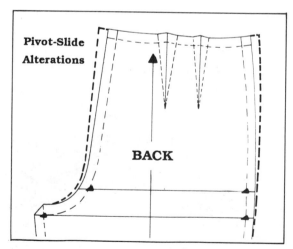

Pivoting has been used for years by fashion designers and sliding is standard for pattern grading. You can use these methods too.

How to Use This Book

Follow this book step-by-step. For best results, read it like a novel, from start to finish, instead of skipping around. Pivot-Slide Alterations follow a series of simple, logical steps:

1. First take measurements and determine your pattern size.
2. Then, prepare your pattern for fitting.
3. Make length alternations in the following order:
   - Fitting the crotch (which includes adjustments for your tummy and seat)
   - Fitting a high hip
   - Fitting length
4. Next make width alterations for:
   - Fitting the waistline
   - Fitting the hipline
   - Fitting the thigh
5. Fine tune your fitting in a trial pair of slacks.
6. Make any needed adjustments
7. Check your fit again and finish your slacks using the "Pivot-Slide Slacks Pattern."

Ease is what I call "living room." Designers add an inch or two of ease or extra room to basic measurements for style and comfort. The amount of ease isn't recorded on the envelope so it's difficult to guess how different patterns will fit — even if they're the same size and style. The enclosed "Pivot-Slide Slacks Pattern" uses the following ease amounts: 3-1/2" ease was added at the hip and 1-1/2" was added at the waist. These standard amounts work well in slacks made from wovens or from knits with less than 25% stretch.

Commercial slack patterns are usually purchased by hip size. My experience shows that most often, while the hip may fit properly, the legs bag like pajamas and the crotch drops toward the knees.

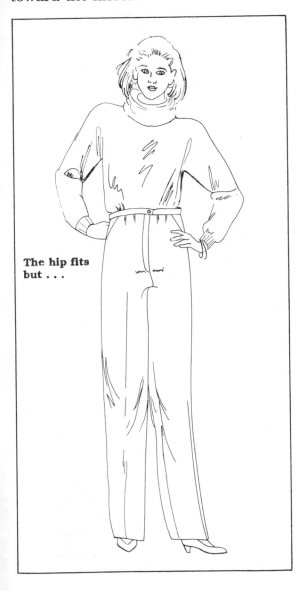

The hip fits but . . .

The enclosed "Pivot-Slide Slacks Pattern" is drafted so the hips, legs, and thighs closely resemble the way we're really built. **With this pattern only, use the size that corresponds to your hip size.**

Measure to Determine Your Size

Don't cheat yourself out of a good fit! Be honest and accurate with your measurements. For best results:
* Dress in a leotard or in your undergarments.
* Work with a partner and fill in the fitting chart.
* Use a fiberglass tape measure and take all measurements over one thumb or finger.

A. Measure the fullest part of your hipline, making sure that the tape measure is parallel with the floor.

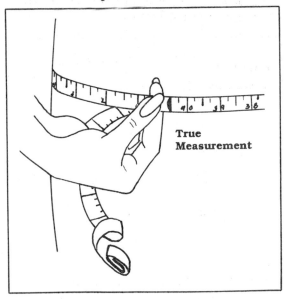

True Measurement

B. Refer to the chart and choose your "Pivot-Slide Slacks" size.

C. Write Hip and Waist Measurements for this pattern size on the Fitting Chart. (See chart.)
Exceptions:
* If your measurement falls between sizes, choose one of the closest sizes. If you legs and thighs are slender use the smaller one. If they are heavy, use the larger one.
* If you have EXTREMELY SLENDER THIGHS, use a smaller size pattern.

* If you hipline is greater than 48", use the 48 pattern.

I never use anything larger than size 48 because larger sizes create legs that are uncontrollably baggy. It's much easier to make the hip area larger than to make all other areas smaller.

* For all three exceptions, you'll need to change the pattern. See how on pages 34-36.

PIVOT-SLIDE SLACKS SIZES

Hip Measurement	34″	36″	38″	40″	42″	44″	46″	48″
Corresponding Waist Measurement	25″	26″	27″	28″	30″	32″	34″	36″

FITTING CHART

	PATTERN MEASUREMENTS –	YOUR MEASUREMENTS =	NEEDED ALTERATION
* HIP			
* WAIST			
CROTCH			
HIGH HIP			
(THIGH)			
LENGTH			

* Fill-in the size which most closely corresponds to your hip measurement, from the Pivot-Slide Slacks Sizes Chart and the corresponding waist measurement.

Prepare Your Basic Pattern
  *Tissue, Freezer, or Waxed Paper
  *Fabric weights or Tape
  *Permanent Marking Pen
  *Tape Measure

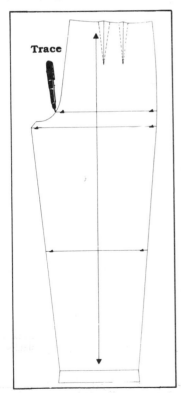 *If the wax paper isn't wide enough, fuse 2 widths of wax paper together for your worksheet paper. Use a dry iron heated to Wool. Trace onto wax paper with a felt tipped pen. You can see through this paper and it's comparably inexpensive.*

1. Trace off the right size onto freezer paper, using a fine point permanent marking pen.
2. Tape or weight your tracing paper and the original pattern together.

Trace

3. Mark the kneeline, crotchline, hipline, hemline, and grainline. You'll notice the grainline goes from top to bottom of each pattern piece. This helps during alterations.
4. Mark the notches, darts, and dots given for your size.
5. Mark 5/8" seam allowances on your pattern worksheet. **Each pattern has 5/8" seams allowed.**

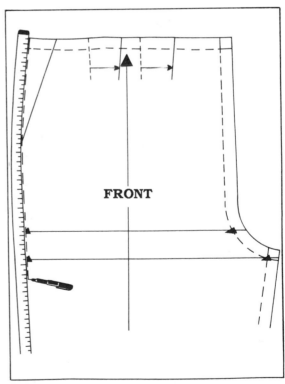 *The easiest way to add a seam allowance is to line up your tape measure along your tracing line and mark along the outer edge of the tape. (Almost all tape measures are 5/8" wide.)*

FRONT

6. Trim your traced pattern along cutting lines.

**7. This is your basic pattern.
DO NOT CUT OUT FABRIC YET.**

The next step is to check the pattern measurements against your measurements.

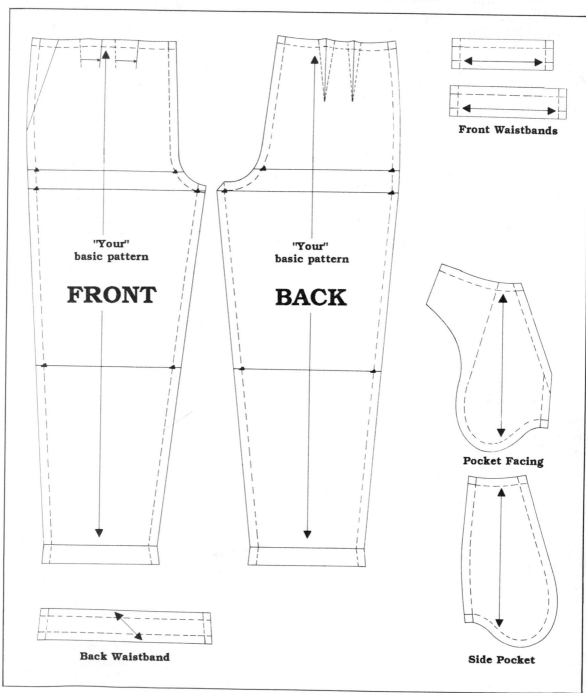

Front Waistbands

"Your"
basic pattern

FRONT

"Your"
basic pattern

BACK

Pocket Facing

Back Waistband

Side Pocket

Group like activities together to keep your fitting simple. Start by doing all lengthening alterations. In Chapter 2, you'll fit all length areas: the crotch, high hip, and the length.

When you alter for length using the Pivot-Slide method, you Slide the pattern up or down along the grain-line as you would raise or lower a window. Make all length alterations on a worksheet. A worksheet is another length of freezer paper, tissue paper, or two lengths of wax paper fused together and placed under your basic slacks pattern.

As you make changes to the original pattern, jot down what you've done and why. That way if you have to put down and pick up your sewing you won't waste time wondering what you did.

Alteration Unit 1: Fitting the Crotch

Probably the most difficult area in fitting slacks is the crotch. You'll be working to get your curves to fit the pattern curves. If you do a good job, the finished pants will lie smooth; if

not, you'll get wrinkles, or the slacks won't hang right around your middle.

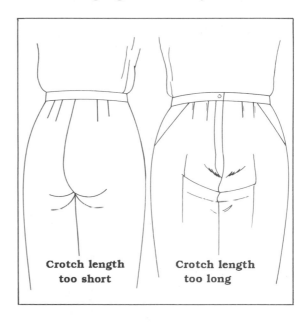

Crotch length too short   Crotch length too long

Measuring the Crotch

Accurate crotch measurements are critical to a good fit in slacks. Start and stop your crotch measurement where your slacks actually rest.

1. Use the top of your hip bone, known as your "shelf" <u>not your waistline</u> for the starting point. (The waistband seam rests at the top of your hipbone, not your waistline.)

13

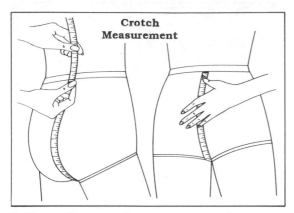

Crotch Measurement

2. Run the tape between your legs and stop at the deepest part of the sway in your back. Take this measurement just the way you want your slacks to fit, not too tight or too loose.

3. Write this measurement on the Fitting Chart, page 10.

Measuring the Pattern

1. Pin front and back together at the crotch seam, stacking stitching lines.

2. Place the end of the tape measure at the seam line at the center front. Stand the tape measure on edge and "walk" it around the seamline to the center back seamline.

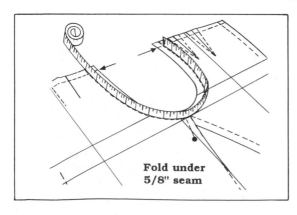

Fold under 5/8" seam

3. Write the pattern measurement on the Fitting Chart page. Add or subtract the difference between your measurement and the pattern measurement.

4. Place a worksheet, a length of tissue paper, freezer paper, or two lengths of wax paper, under the pattern. Outline the entire pattern on your worksheet following the cutting line.

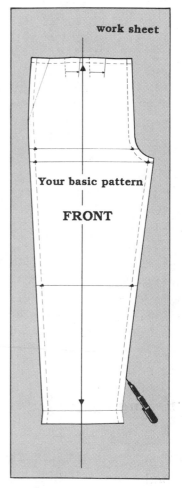

work sheet

Your basic pattern

FRONT

5. Mark the grainline. Extend the grainline above and below the pattern on your worksheet.

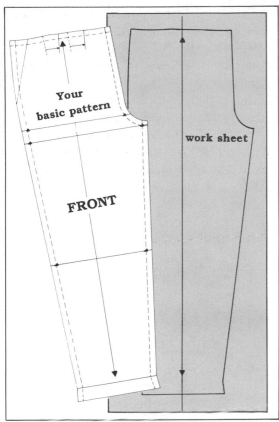

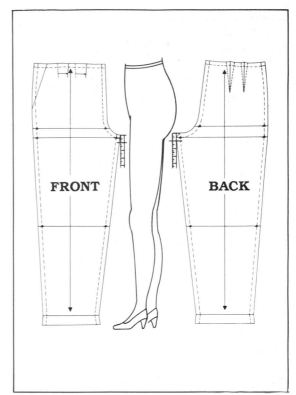

6. Determine how much the crotch will be lengthened or shortened. **If the alteration is 4" or less, changes will be made at each crotch point. If the alteration is 4" or more, changes will be made at each crotch point, as well as at center front and/or center back.**

Lengthening the Crotch 4" or Less

In most cases the crotch will be lengthened or shortened by 4" or less. The alteration is divided by 2 and the changes are added evenly on the front and back.

Slack patterns are drafted the way most of us are shaped—a slight curve in the front and a fuller curve in the back. The back pattern is 2-3" longer than the front to accommodate for sitting room.

1. Divide the increase by 2.
2. On the worksheet, measure **DOWN** from each crotch cutting line the amount determined in Step 1. Mark on the worksheet.
3. Place the pattern on the work sheet. Slide the pattern **DOWN** along the grainline until the pattern's cutting line meets the alteration mark. Draw in the longer crotch and the changed portion of the inseam.

15

4. Mark this longer crotchline on the **worksheet**. Since the crotch has been lowered, the horizontal line has also been lowered. The crotchline is marked 5/8" below the new crotch point cutting line.

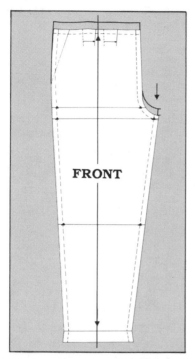

FRONT

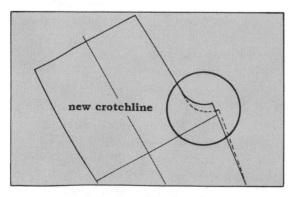

Use a different color permanent marking pen or a dotted line to show the difference between the original outline and the new outline.

new crotchline

5. Repeat with back pattern piece.

Shortening the Crotch 4" or Less

1. Divide the decrease by 2.
2. On the worksheet, measure **UP** from each crotch cutting line the amount determined in Step A. Mark on the worksheet.
3. Place that pattern over the worksheet. Slide the pattern **UP** along the grainline until the pattern's cutting line meets the alteration mark. Draw the shorter crotch and the changed portion of the inseam.

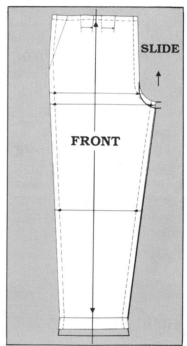

SLIDE

FRONT

4. Mark a new crotchline on the **worksheet**. Since the crotch has been raised, the horizontal line has also been raised. The new crotch line is marked 5/8" below the new crotch point cutting line.

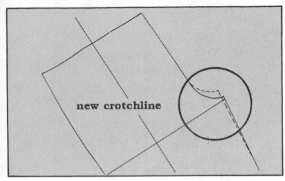

new crotchline

5. Repeat with back pattern piece.

Lengthening the Crotch 4" or More

If the crotch needs to be lengthened 4" or more you'll make part of the alteration at the crotch point and part at the center front and/or center back. This helps fit the crotch closer to your figure. You know your figure better than anyone else, so consider all three possibilities and choose the way that best fits you.

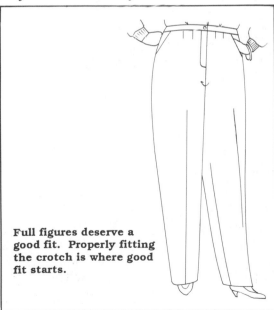

Full figures deserve a good fit. Properly fitting the crotch is where good fit starts.

Possibility #1: Full Figure

Use this alteration if you have both a rounded tummy AND a predominant curve in your seat.

Step 1: Determine How Much To Add and Where

A. Divide the needed increase by 4.
B. Add 1" above the cutting line at center front.
C. Add 1" above the cutting line at center back.
D. Divide the remaining increase between crotch points on front and back.

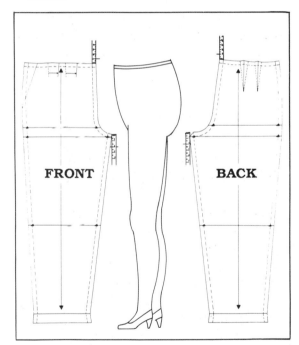

FRONT   BACK

Step 2: Mark Alteration Points On The Front Pattern Worksheet

A. Mark points determined in Step 1.

For example, if 6" more are needed: Mark 1" **above** the original outline at the center front. Mark 1" **above** the original outline at the center back. Mark 2" **below** the outline at each crotchline.

B. Lengthen crotch by sliding pattern **DOWN** along the grainline to new crotch mark. Draw in lower part of new crotchline and the changed portion of the inseam.

C. Add length at waist by sliding pattern **UP** along the grainline to the new center front mark. Draw in the longer crotchline

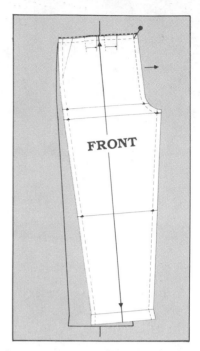

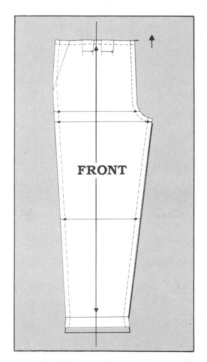

D. At center front, place a pin at the waistline where stitching lines cross.

E. Pivot the pattern so it meets the outline at this side seam. Draw new waistline.

Step 3: Repeat Alterations On The Back Pattern Piece

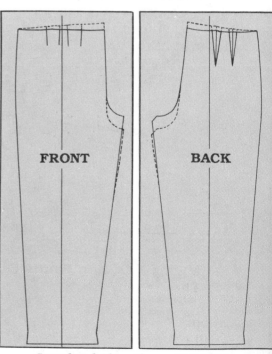

Completed Alterations – Full Figure

Possibility #2: Predominant Tummy

If your figure has a larger curve in the tummy area and not so much curve in the seat, this is the alteration for you.

Step 1: Determine How Much to Add and Where

A. Divide the needed increase by 3.
B. Add 1" above cutting line at center front.
C. Divide remaining increase between crotch points on both front and back.

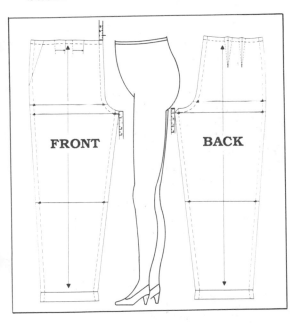

Step 2: Mark Alteration Points On The Front Pattern Piece

A. Mark points determined in Step 1. You will not change the center back at the waist. For example, if 5" more is needed: Mark 1" **above** the outline at the center front. Mark 2" **below** the outline at each crotchline.

B. Follow Steps B through E under Step 2 for **Possibility #1: Full Figure.**

Step 3: Repeat Alterations on the Back Pattern Piece

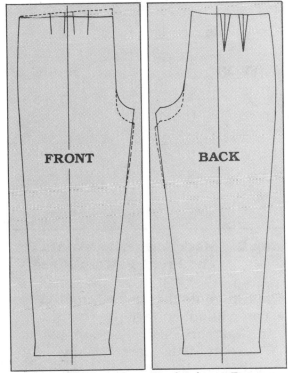

Completed Alteration – Predominant Tummy

Possibility # 3: Predominant Seat

If your figure has a greater curve in the seat area or if you notice that your slacks "pull down" in the back when sitting, you need this alteration.

Step 1: Determine How Much to Add and Where

A. Add 1" above waist at center back.
B. Divide remaining increase between front and back crotch points.

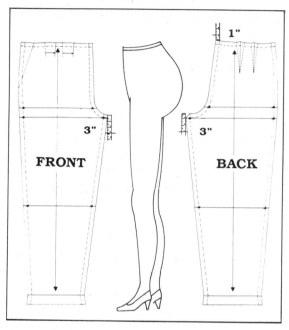

Step 2: Mark Alteration Points On The Front Pattern Piece

A. Mark points determined in Step 1. You will not change the center front at the waist. For example, if 7" are needed: Mark 1" **above** the outline at the center back. Mark 3" **below** the outline at each crotchline.
B. Follow B - E under Step 2 for **Possibility #1: Full Figure.**

Step 3: Repeat Alterations On The Back Pattern Piece

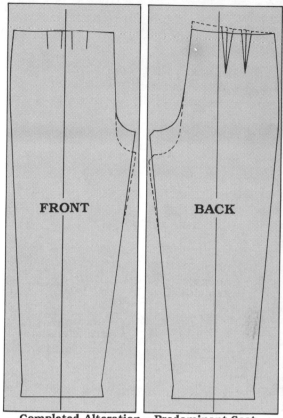

Completed Alteration – Predominant Seat

Make certain the new crotchline is marked on the worksheet. The crotchline is marked 5/8" below the new crotch point cutting line.

Review: Fitting the Crotch

When using Pivot-Slide Alterations, wrinkles under the seat are removed by sliding the pattern **DOWN** to lengthen the crotch and/or adding length at center front and center back. Other methods add a "piece of pie" at the back crotch making the thigh wider but not actually changing the crotch length.

When using Pivot-Slide Alterations, a low crotch is solved by sliding the crotch **UP** along the grainline. This is more accurate than folding out a tuck which can shift the grainline or create uneven side seams.

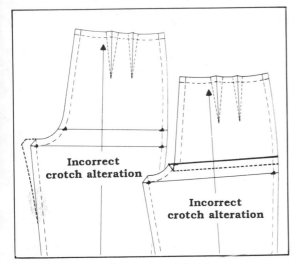

Alteration Unit 2: Fitting a High or Low Hip

Most of us are concerned with the number of inches around our figure. But the hip's curve and shape is also extremely important. The greater the curve, the more length on the slack's side seams. A high-curvy hip will need more side length than average; a low-flat hip will need less.

How your slacks fit at the hips affects how the creases hang. If the side seam is too long, your creases may hang inward. If the side seam is too short your creases may bow outward. It's also very common for one hip to be higher than the other, causing one crease to hang straight and one to bow outward.

An alteration for high hips must be made before cutting out your pattern. It's easier, though, to fit a low hip during the first fitting by shortening the side length.

Measuring the High Hip Length

You'll measure the high hip length at your side "shelf," measuring below your waistline but above your hip-bone where your slacks actually rest.

1. Place an elastic strip sewn in a circle on your leg to show your crotchline (or refer to your brief-style panty line.)
2. Find your shelf by placing your thumbs at your sides.
3. Measure from your shelf to your panty line to the closest 1/4".
4. Record your measurement on the Fitting Chart, page 10.

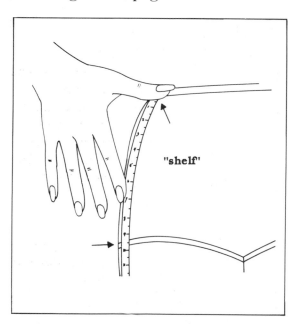

"shelf"

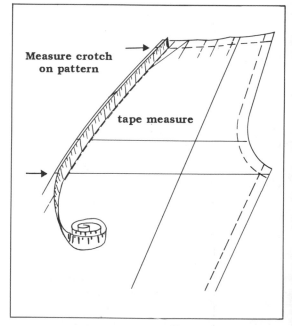 *Measure both hip lengths and use the longer measurement if there is a difference.*

Measuring the Pattern—on the Worksheet

Before you measure the high hip length, check to see if you re-drew the crotchline on the **worksheet** after making any changes in the crotch during Unit 1 Alterations.

Then measure the high hip length on the **front worksheet** piece:

1. Stand the the tape measure on its side. Start measuring 5/8" from the waist cutting line.
2. Walk the tape measure down to your crotchline marked on the worksheet.

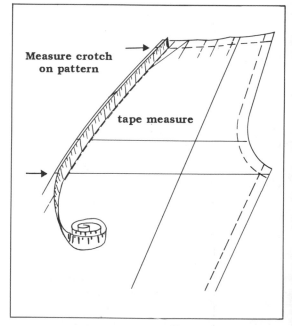

Measure crotch on pattern

tape measure

3. Write measurement on the Fitting Chart.
4. Determine how much to add (difference between your measurement and the pattern).

Only alter to add hip length. If you need to take out some length in the hip area for one (or both) hips, you'll do that later-during the first fitting. See page 55.

Altering for a High Hip Length

1. Place worksheet under front pattern piece.
2. Mark a point **above** the outline on the worksheet at the side waistline for the needed addition.

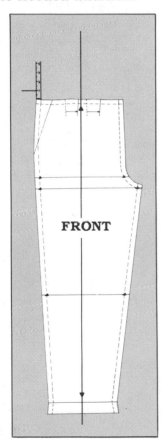

3. Slide the pattern **UP,** following the grainline until the cutting line meets this mark.

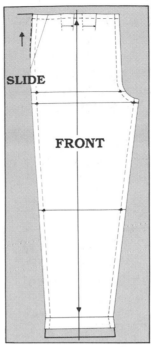

4. Draw in the longer side seam.

5. Place a pin where the side seam and waistline cross.

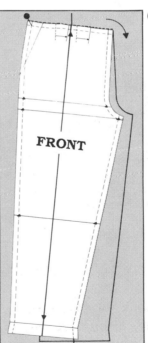

6. Pivot your pattern so that the center front waistline seam meets the original outline on the worksheet.

7. Draw in the new waist cutting line.

8. Repeat steps 1-7 on back pattern piece.

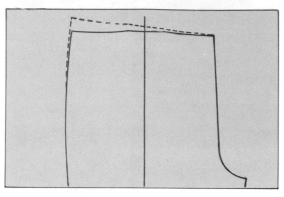

Review: Fitting the High Hip

Patterns are altered at the side only to add length for a higher hip. This length is added on both front and back at the side seam. Any changes for extra length will be pinned out and trimmed away during the first fitting.

Alteration Unit 3: Fitting the Length

Changing the length of slacks is the easiest alteration. Try using the Pivot-Slide method instead of folding or slashing. By Sliding the pattern you will not disrupt the side seams or the grainline.

Measuring the Length

You can take this measurement over a pair of slacks.

1. Have your partner measure the side seam from your "shelf" to the finished length.
2. Write the measurement on the Fitting Chart, page 10.

Measuring the Pattern

Measure your basic pattern starting with the Front pattern piece.
1. Stand the tape measure on its side with one end at the 5/8" seamline at the side seam.
2. Walk the tape measure down the side seam to the hemline.

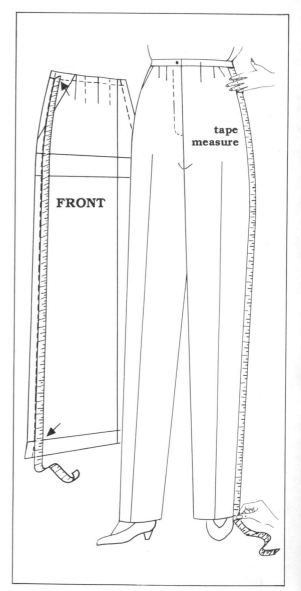

FRONT

tape measure

3. Write this measurement on the Fitting Chart.
4. Determine how much to add or subtract (the difference between your measurement and the pattern).

If you altered for a longer High Hip, be sure to measure your worksheet pattern instead of the original pattern.

Lengthen the Slacks

1. On your worksheet, measure **DOWN** from the bottom outline the needed addition and make a mark.

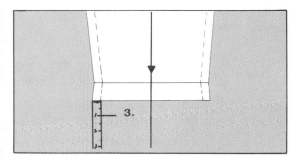

2. Slide your pattern **DOWN** on the worksheet, following the grainline, until you reach the new mark.
3. Draw a dotted line for the new hem and side seam.

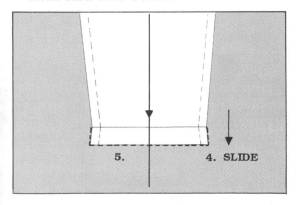

Shorten the Slacks

1. On your worksheet, measure **UP** from the bottom outline and make a mark.

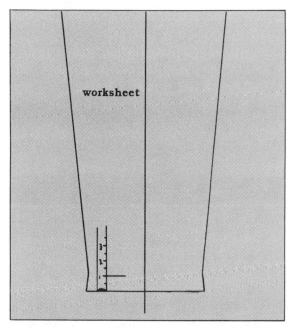

2. Slide your pattern **UP** on the worksheet, following the grainline until you reach the new mark.

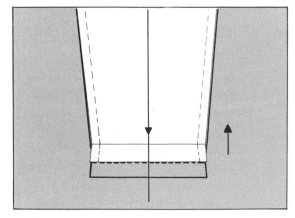

3. Draw a dotted line for the new hem and side seam.

Review: Lengthening or Shortening the Hemline

Instead of tucking or slashing your pattern, slide the pattern up or down to draw a new hemline. This method is easier and much more accurate than other methods.

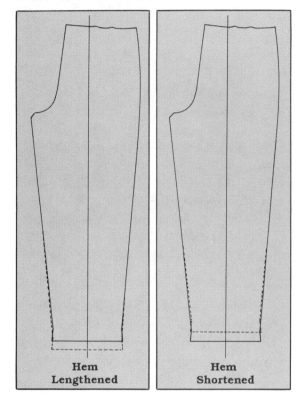

| Hem Lengthened | Hem Shortened |

Pivoting works like the swing of a pendulum, to add or subtract from your pattern's width. You'll start by anchoring your pattern at an ALTERATION POINT, then swing it wider or narrower as needed. ALTERATION POINTS are marked on the "Pivot-Slide Slacks Pattern" with triangles. You'll use these alteration areas:

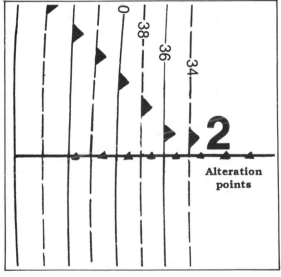

* The hip alteration point at the stitching line is used to increase or decrease the waistline. (A very common alteration.)
* The crotch alteration point and the knee alteration points are used to increase the thigh and hip.

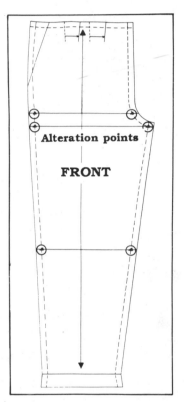

Alteration Unit 4: Fitting the Waistline

Three basic width measurement include: waist, hip and thigh.
If your hip measurement is 48" or less, the enclosed "Pivot-Slide Slacks Pattern" is already altered to fit your hip and thigh. If your hip or thigh are larger than the basic pattern, we will check the pattern after fitting the waistline.

Measure the Waistline

1. Place the tape measure around the smallest part of your waistline. (Bend to the side, the deepest wrinkle is your waist.)
2. Measure over one finger or thumb to the closest 1/2".
3. Write this measurement on the Fitting Chart, page 10.

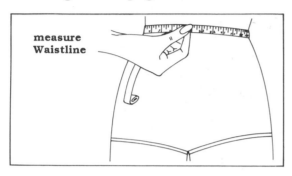

measure
Waistline

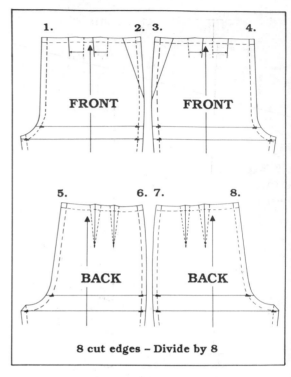

8 cut edges – Divide by 8

Compare with the Pattern Measurement

1. Look on the Fitting Chart for the waist measurement of your basic pattern.
2. Determine the difference to add or subtract.
3. **DIVIDE YOUR NEEDED ALTERATION BY 8.** Yes, 8. There are eight cut edges on the four seams.

Use a calculator or this fraction trick:

Place the needed number over 8 in a fraction. For example, to add 5" to the waist. You would add 5/8" at each cut edge. If you needed 3" more, you'd add 3/8" at each cut edge. (Easy, isn't it?)

Increase the Waistline

1. On your worksheet, measure <u>out</u> from both sides of the waist cutting lines the needed increase. Mark on the worksheet.

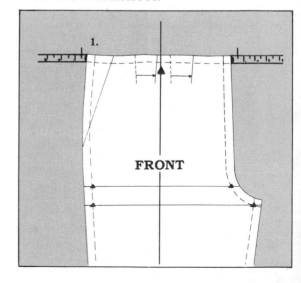

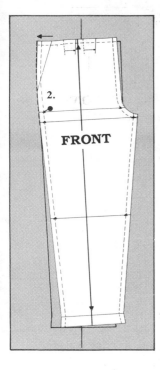

2. Line up your pattern and the worksheet. Place a pin at waist alteration point, the stitching line of the hip.

3. **PIVOT** your pattern so the cutting line meets the increase mark. Draw a new cutting line between the waist and hip.

4. Line up pattern and worksheet again. Place a pin at the other waist alteration point, the inner stitching line of the hip. **PIVOT** pattern and draw a new cutting line between hip and waist.

5. Extend waist cutting line across top of pattern.

6. Repeat steps 1-5 on other slacks pattern piece.

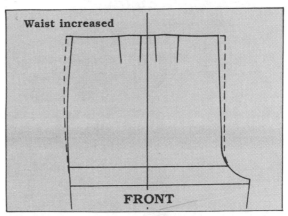

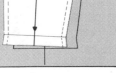 **If you altered for a High Hip, extend the waistline increase to include this change.**

Decrease the Waistline

1. On your worksheet, measure **in** from both sides of the waist cutting line. Mark on the worksheet.

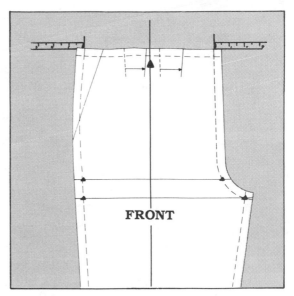

2. Line up your pattern and the worksheet. Place a pin at the waist alteration point, the stitching line of the hip.

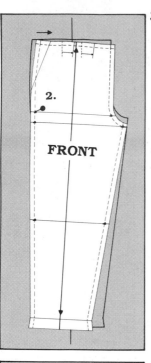

3. **PIVOT** the pattern until the waist cutting line meets the decrease mark. Draw in a new cutting line between hip and waist.

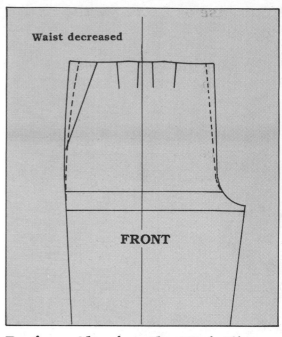

Review: Altering the Waistline

Using this method you alter evenly on both sides of the waist leaving darts and grainline unchanged. Other methods add or subtract only on the outside seam changing the dart and tipping the grainline.

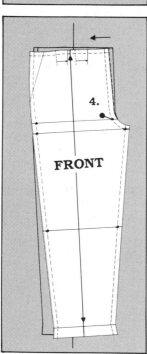

4. Line up pattern and worksheet again. Place a pin at the other waist alteration point, the inner stitching line of the hip. **PIVOT** the pattern until the waist cutting line meets the decrease mark. Draw in new cutting line between hip and waist.

5. Repeat steps 1-4 on other slacks pattern piece.

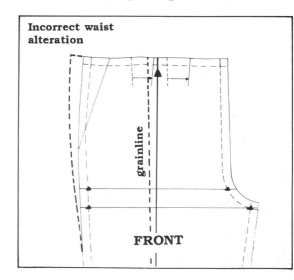

Increase or Decrease the Waistband

Changing the waistline necessitates a change in the waistband, like this:

1. Divide your needed increase or decrease by 4. (This waistband has 2 side seams or 4 cut edges.)

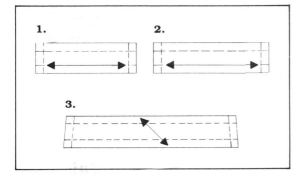

2. Since the waistband is seamed at the side, alter the back piece on both sides. Alter the front only at the side seam.
   For example: To add 4" to the waistband, add 1" to front side seam and 1" at **each** of the back side seams.

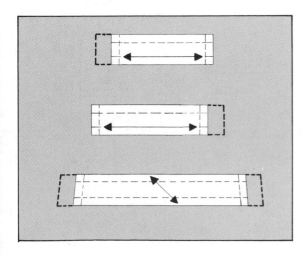

This pattern has been drafted to fit hip and thighs. In most cases, you won't need to check these areas and can skip to Chapter 4. But if you are using a smaller size because of slender thighs or if your hipline is larger than 48", refer to the next two alteration units.

Alteration Unit 5: Fitting the Hipline

I never recommend using a commercial pattern larger than size 20 or size 48 in our "Pivot-Slide Slacks Pattern." The larger sizes include extremely full legs that are both unattractive and uncomfortable. Instead, I recommend changing the hipline without changing leg fullness. Here's how:

1. Write your hip measurement on the Fitting Chart.
2. Determine the amount to add (the difference between your measurement and the pattern, size 48).
3. Divide the needed increase by <u>8</u>. (Like the waistline, there are 8 cut edges per the 4 seams.)

Make a Second Worksheet

1. Start a **second worksheet**. Use your first worksheet as the pattern. Transfer kneeline, crotchline, and hipline to first worksheet. (Set aside original pattern.)
2. Cut out the first worksheet. Pay special attention to the alterations,

31

making sure you are trimming along dotted lines.

3. Layer first worksheet (pattern) over clean worksheet paper. Trace the outline of your pattern.

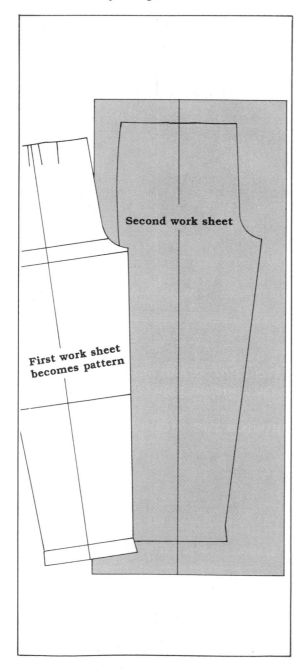

Increasing the Hipline

1. On the worksheet, measure and mark the needed increase on both sides of the hipline.

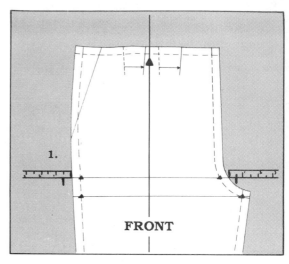

2. Line up pattern and new worksheet. Place a pin at the hip **alteration point**, the stitching line at the knee.

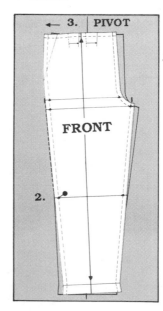

3. **PIVOT** pattern so hip cutting line meets your mark. Draw a dotted line to show the new cutting line.

4. KEEP THE PATTERN PIVOTED. Remove pin and place it at hip stitching line.

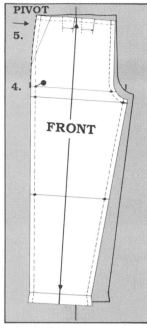

5. **PIVOT** pattern to original outline at waist. Draw new cutting line between hip and waist.

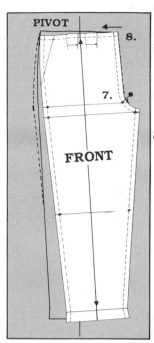

7. KEEP THE PATTERN PIVOTED. Remove pin and place it at hip stitching line.

8. **PIVOT** pattern to original outline at waist. Draw new cutting line between hip and waist.

9. Repeat steps 1-8 on other slacks piece.

6. Line up pattern and worksheet. Place a pin at the other hip alteration point, the inner stitching line of the knee. **PIVOT** pattern so the hip cutting line meets increase mark. Draw new cutting line between hip and waist.

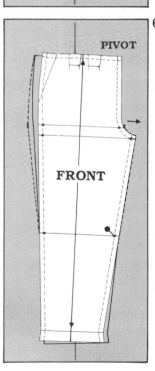

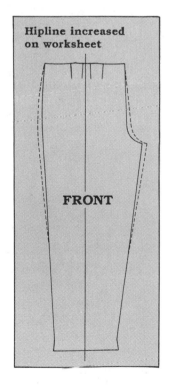

Hipline increased on worksheet

This hipline alteration keeps the leg attractive, gradually adding width where it's needed-— at the hips.

Alteration Unit 6: Fitting the Thigh

In the "Pivot-Slide Slacks Pattern" extra ease was allowed so that the back crease of the slacks would hang straight from the fullest part of the seat. Jeans, in contrast, fit snugly in the thigh.

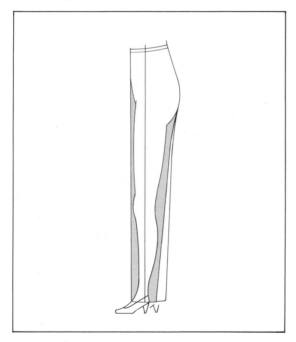

Figures with full thighs require 2" of ease at the hipline. But figures with _small thighs and full hips_ require additional room for slacks to hang properly. The greater the difference between hip and thigh, the more ease will be needed in the thigh.

Increase the Thigh

A. Measure fullest part of upper leg.
  * Add 2" for ease. (Average recommended for full thighs.)
  * Record this measurement on the Fitting Chart, page 10.

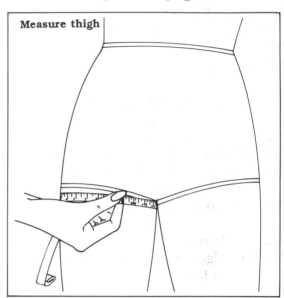

Measure thigh

B. If you increased the hipline, check the thigh measurement on the **worksheet.** If the hipline was not altered, check the thigh measurement on the basic pattern.

If you altered the hipline, mark the stitching lines on the worksheet. Any time you are marking a seam line, place one side of the tape measure along the cutting line and trace the other side of the tape. Almost all tape measures are 5/8" wide.

C. Measure the width of the thigh (directly below crotchline) between sewing lines.

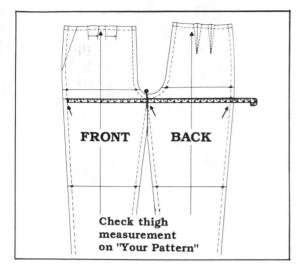

Check thigh
measurement
on "Your Pattern"

D. Write this measurement on the Fitting Chart. Add the difference between this measurement and the pattern measurement.

E. Divide needed increase by 4 (four cut edges per 2 seams in each slacks leg).

Alter Your Pattern

1. On the worksheet, measure and mark the needed increase on *both* sides of the crotch outline.

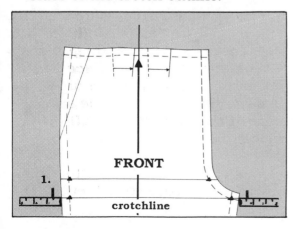

FRONT

1.

crotchline

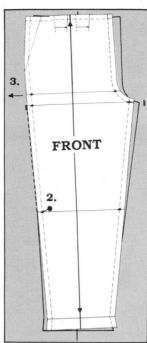

FRONT

3.

2.

2. Line up pattern and worksheet. Place a pin at the crotch Alteration Point, the stitching line of the knee *on the outside seam.*

3. **PIVOT** pattern so thigh cutting line meets your increase mark. With a dotted line, draw in new cutting line.

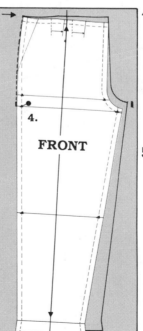

FRONT

4.

4. KEEP THE PATTERN PIVOTED. Remove the pin from the knee and place it at the crotch's stitching line.

5. **PIVOT** pattern to meet outline of hipline. Draw new cutting line between crotch and hip.

6. Return pattern to original position.

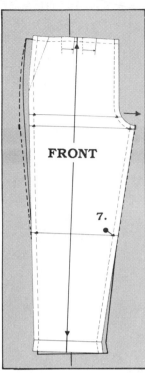

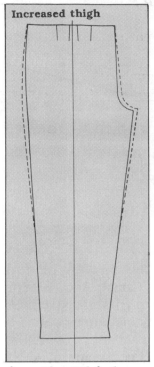

Increased thigh

7. Place pin at other Alteration Point, *inner* stitching line of knee. **PIVOT** pattern so thigh cutting line meets increase mark. Draw new dotted cutting line between knee and crotch.

8. KEEP THE PATTERN PIVOTED. Remove pin from knee and place at crotch point stitching lines.

9. **PIVOT** pattern to meet outline of hipline. Draw new cutting line between crotch and hip.

10. Repeat steps 1-9 on Back pattern piece.

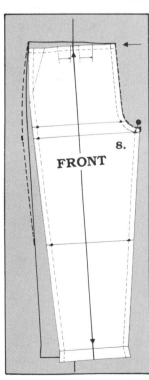

Decreasing the Thigh

A. Measure fullest part of upper leg. Record measurement on the Fitting Chart, page 10.

B. Measure width of thigh on pattern.

C. Measure the width of the thigh (directly below crotchline) between sewing lines.

D. Record this measurement.

E. Compare pattern measurement with your measurement. If the difference is 5" or more, the pattern should be decreased in the thigh. For example: If your measurement in Step A is 16" and the pattern measures 23. Subtract 16 from 23 = 7. To make this difference = 5, you will **decrease your thigh by 2"**.

F. Divide needed decrease by 4 (four cut edges in 2 leg seams).

Alter the Pattern

1. Trace pattern cutting line on worksheet.

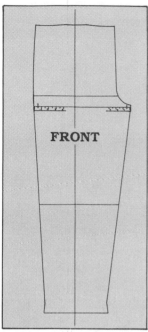

2. On the worksheet, measure **in** from the cutting line of crotch the needed decrease and mark.

3. Line up pattern on worksheet. Place a pin at the crotch Alteration Point, the stitching line of knee *on the outside seam.*

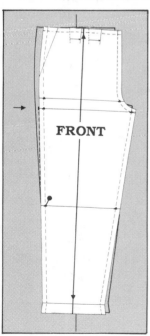

4. **PIVOT** pattern so cutting line meets decrease mark. Draw in a new dotted cutting line between knee and thigh.

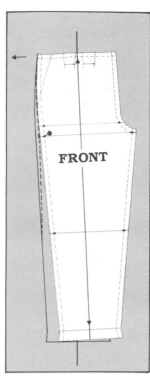

5. KEEP THE PATTERN PIVOTED. Remove pin from knee and place at crotch stitching line.

6. **PIVOT** pattern to meet hipline. Draw in new dotted cutting line between crotch and hip.

7. Return pattern to original position.

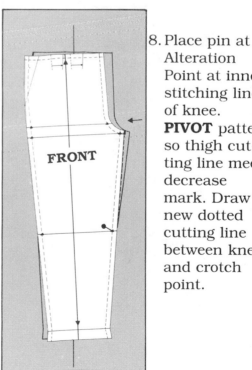

8. Place pin at Alteration Point at inner stitching line of knee. **PIVOT** pattern so thigh cutting line meets decrease mark. Draw in new dotted cutting line between knee and crotch point.

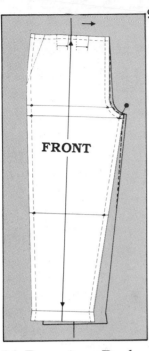

9. KEEP THE PATTERN PIVOTED. Remove pin from knee and place at crotch point.

10. **PIVOT** pattern to meet outline of hip. Draw in new cutting line between crotch and hip.

Review of Pivot Alterations

Waist, hip and crotch alterations are very similar. Inches are added or subtracted by pivoting on both sides of the grainline allowing gradual changes.

11. Repeat on Back pattern piece.

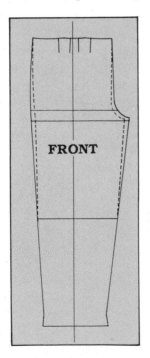

Worksheet Becomes Your Personalized Pattern

During alterations you made changes in the original pattern on a work-sheet. This worksheet is now your PERSONALIZED PATTERN.

Use your worksheet when cutting out your fabric. Double check to be sure the darts, notches, and dots of your basic pattern were transferred to the worksheet.

To cut fabric easily, trim along the cutting lines of your worksheet. Be sure to trim on dotted lines and pay special attention to altered areas.

IMPORTANT: FLY FRONT EXTENSION

Your "Pivot-Slide Slacks Pattern" is designed with a fly front zipper. Trace your size Fly Front Extension and tape to pattern, matching dots and lining up the cutting line of the front over the cutting line of the Extension.

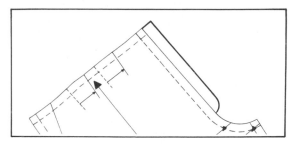

Side Pockets — Pattern Changes (Optional)

To have Side Pockets, your front pattern piece will be cut to accommo-date two pocket pieces:

A. Using wax paper, tissue, or freezer paper, trace off your size pocket facing and pocket insert. DO NOT TRIM along the cutting lines. Leave excess paper around pattern pieces.

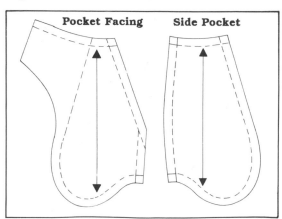

Pocket Facing   Side Pocket

B. If you altered at the waist or hip, the pocket pieces must also be changed. Fold and pin pleats on slacks front as if they were sewn. Place Pocket Facing over pattern, matching notches #1 and #2 and the center front with the *original* center front tracing line on pattern. Draw changes at waist, side seam, and center front.

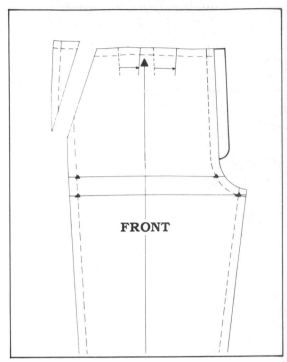

FRONT

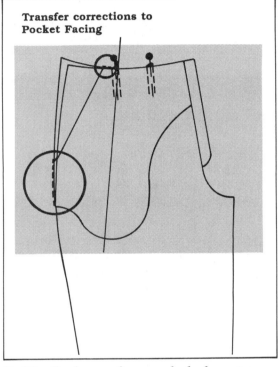

Transfer corrections to Pocket Facing

Leg Width Changes

Finished leg width of the "Pivot-Slide Slacks Pattern" is printed on the Sizing Chart. If you want to change the width:

C. Similarly, make needed changes on Side Pocket. There will be changes at side or waist, not at center front.

D. On altered Front pattern, use the side pocket cutting line for your size. Cut pattern along this line. **Save the wedge shape for making pants without pockets at a later date.**

1. Determine the difference between the width you want and the width on the pattern. Divide the amount you add or subtract by 4. (4 cut edges per slacks leg.)
2. On worksheet, measure and mark desired change along cut edges of hem. *(Both sides.)*
3. Line up pattern and worksheet. Place pin at sewing line of crotch and PIVOT pattern so cutting line meets increase or decrease mark. Draw new dotted cutting line between crotch and hem. Repeat on other side.

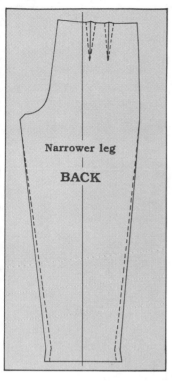

Narrower leg

BACK

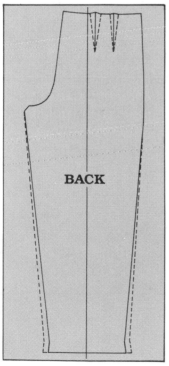

BACK

Fabric Selection and Care

Stitch your new slacks in any stable fabric. Wovens such as chino, cotton blends, gabardine, denim, wool, or corduroy work well. Knits with 25% stretch or less such as ponte, crepe, and double knits are also considered stable fabrics.

Pre-wash fabrics just like you will when they get soiled. I pre-wash my permanent press fabrics with slightly soiled garments as long as fabric contents are compatible. Pre-washing removes resins and starches put in fabrics during the weaving or knitting process (which can cause skipped stitches). It also allows for fabric shrinkage and shows the fabric's true nature.

Layout Instructions

After pre-washing and drying fabrics, refold matching the selvages. Disregard the original fold which may be off-grain.

Always place pattern pieces going the same direction, like you would if the fabric had a nap (directional shading). Sometimes shading can occur on flat surfaced fabrics and won't be noticed until slacks are made.

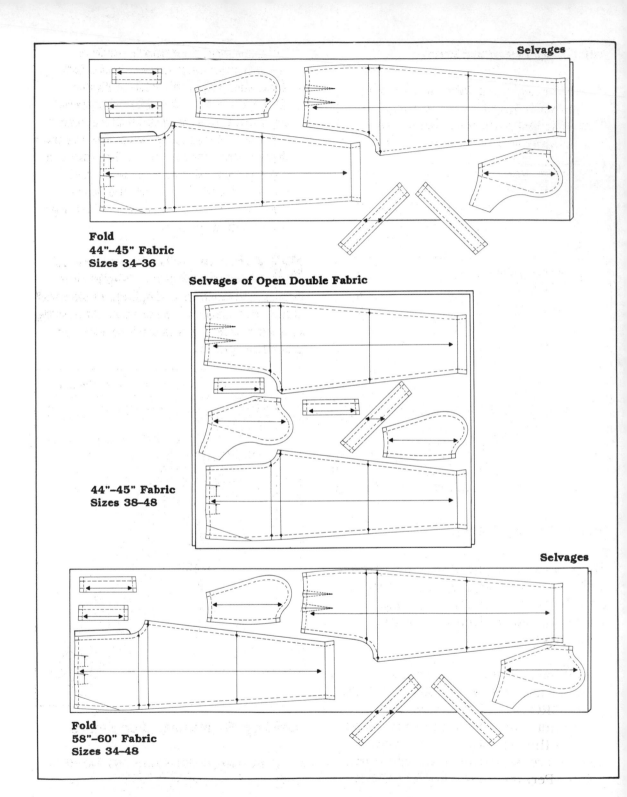

Selvages

Fold
44"–45" Fabric
Sizes 34–36

Selvages of Open Double Fabric

44"–45" Fabric
Sizes 38–48

Selvages

Fold
58"–60" Fabric
Sizes 34–48

Marking Instructions

A. Mark inverted notches and dart legs with "nips," 1/4" clips.
B. Mark dart ends with washable marking pen or pencil.

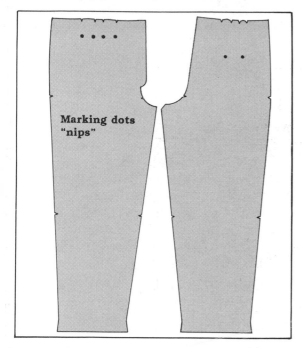

Marking dots
"nips"

Press Front Crease

Establishing the front crease is easier before sewing a stitch! Or try stitching in the crease using a double needle. Like this:

1. Fold each front wrong sides together matching cut edges at HEM and CROTCH. (Other cut edges may not meet because of the shaping of the leg - Don't force them.)
2. Press crease between crotch and hem. Permanently set the crease by pressing 5 seconds with a steam iron and press cloth. Lift iron and POUND with a Tailor Clapper® (9" x 2-1/2" hardwood specially designed to flatten and crease). Pounding with the clapper forces out moisture and creates a sharp, long-lasting crease. Let slacks front dry 5 -10 minutes. Press in the back crease after legs are sewn together.

I like to make two pairs of slacks at once. While the front creases are drying, a second pair can also be pressed. It really doesn't take too much longer to sew two pairs.

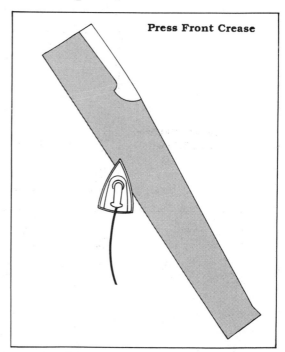

Press Front Crease

Sewing Shortcuts For Darts

Straight darts don't have to be difficult!

1. Match dart nips and fold darts in half, **with dart point on fold.**
2. Pull thread so you have a 12" tail.
3. Place needle in fabric directly below dart nips. Pull thread up to top of fabric to use as a sewing guide.
4. Lower presser foot and stitch dart.

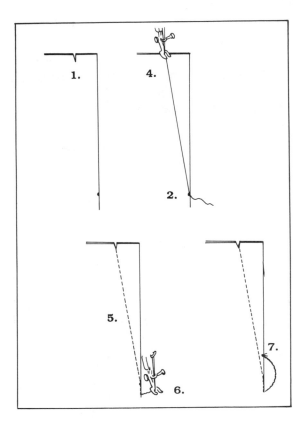

5. When you reach the dart point, sew 3 extra stitches catching just the very edge of fabric.
6. Keep stitching after you run off the fabric letting the thread lock or tie itself.
7. Raise presser foot and pull dart foward. About 1" back from dart point, sew 2-3 lock stitches inside dart.

8. Pull dart to back of machine and clip threads.
9. Press dart underlays toward center front.

Side Pocket — Sewing Instructions

Side pockets are both fashionable and useful. These specially designed pockets have an extension which prevents the pocket from pulling out of shape or creating a bulge at the pleats or tucks.

1. Cut two Side Pockets and two Pocket Facings of fashion fabric.
2. Fuse 1" strip of interfacing to wrong side of pocket area. Or, cut a length of twill tape or Stay Tape™ the length of pattern piece. Stitch the tape to the wrong side along the 5/8" seamline.

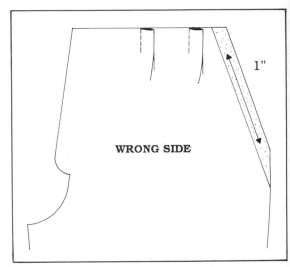

Stay Tape™ is 100% nylon stabilizing tape. Since it's 100% nylon, it does not have to be pre-shrunk prior to using.

3. With right sides together, stitch Pocket Facing to slacks front. Press. Grade seam allowances with pocket seams being narrowest.

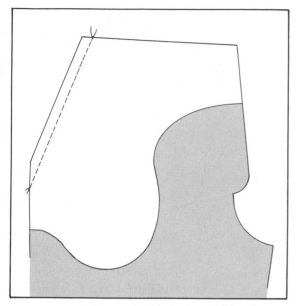

4. Understitch, sewing seam allowance to facing to prevent facing from rolling to outside.

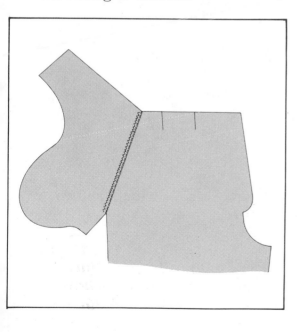

I prefer to use a multi-zigzag or wide zigzag stitch for understitching. These stitches give more stitches/inch, creating a tailored edge. I use this unconventional form of understitching on most woven fabrics and even on knits to prevent the seam allowances from curling.

5. With right sides together, sew pocket to facing. Clean finish edges with zigzag or serged stitch. Fold pocket facing to the wrong side. Zigzag pocket facing to the slacks at the center front and side seam.

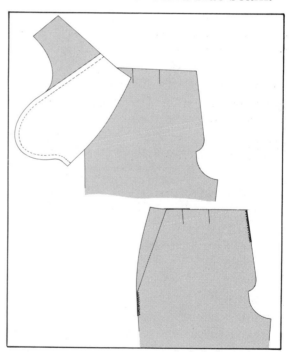

Sewing Seams — Professional Hints

Sewing side seams may appear simple and they are easy. Use these hints to get a better fit and a professional look.

1. Right sides together, sew front and back legs together at the outer side seam. Press the seam flat to straighten the stitches and then press it open over a sleeve roll to prevent the seam edges from leaving an imprint on the right side.

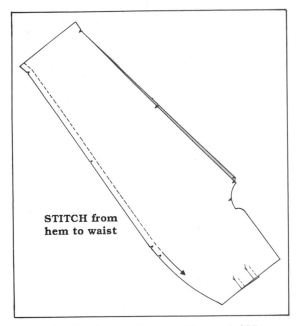

STITCH from hem to waist

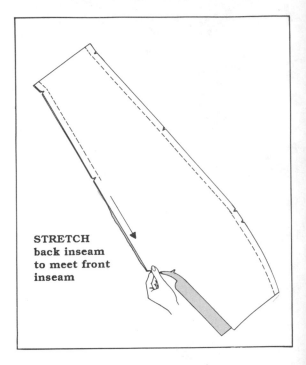

STRETCH back inseam to meet front inseam

2. This slacks pattern allows 1/2" more fabric on the front inseam than the back inseam for sitting ease. Since the back crotch area is curved, it forms a bias which stretches as you ease the back to the front. In turn, this simple easing will give you a smoother fit in the back thigh and extra fabric in the front leg for sitting ease.

3. Match cut edges at hem to knee. Sew from the hem to knee with raw edges meeting perfectly. At the knee, stretch the back inseam to meet the front inseam and continue to sew the remaining half of the inseam.

Always sew with the longer seam (slacks front) next to the feed dogs. The feed dogs will "bite" or automatically ease the fabric while the presser foot stretches the fabric.

Press Back Crease

Before stitching the crotch seam, press back crease:

1. Press the seam allowance using the sleeve roll. Turn each leg rightside out.
2. Fold the slacks along the pressed front crease and anchor the front crease with a sleeve board or other sewing/pressing tool to prevent the slacks from shifting while you press. Press back crease from the hem to the crotch.

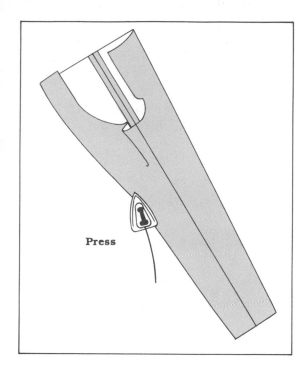

Press

Near the crotch area, the fabric will naturally fold, forming an "inch pinch." Press the back crease, allowing this inch pinch to form in the crotch area. Use a Tailor Clapper® to set the crease. Allow slacks to dry.

This "inch pinch" is ambiguous, but naturally forms in the back inner thigh. The front of the slacks remain flat. Remember to start pressing at the hem and work toward the crotch.

Fly Front Zipper

Zippers are usually placed in the center front or center back seams, not at the side seam, since our hipline curves make side seam zippers buckle or bulge.

1. For the standard 8" zipper opening, purchase a 9" zipper.

I always buy a longer zipper than the zipper opening. Put the extra length at the top and stitch in place. You won't have that bulky zipper pull in your way, which often creates a crooked seam.

2. Mark the center fronts with "nips" On the topside, mark center lines with washable marking pen. On wrong side, mark zipper stop point 1/2" above bottom extension. If you can not remember which side is right or left, mark "R" and "L" on topside with washable pen.

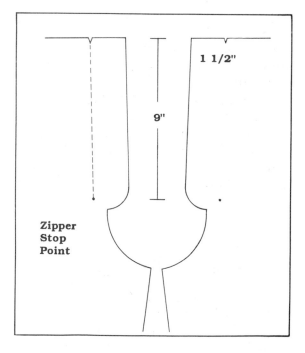

1 1/2"

9"

Zipper
Stop
Point

3. Insert one leg into the other, right sides together. Sew crotch seam ending at zipper stop point.

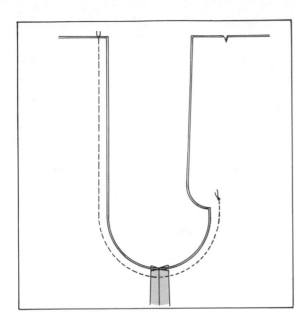

5. Place zipper under LEFT front extension. Position bottom zipper staple directly below zipper opening. Zipper tape will extend above waistline. Place fabric fold about 1/8" from zipper teeth. Stitch fabric to zipper tape using zipper foot. Close zipper.

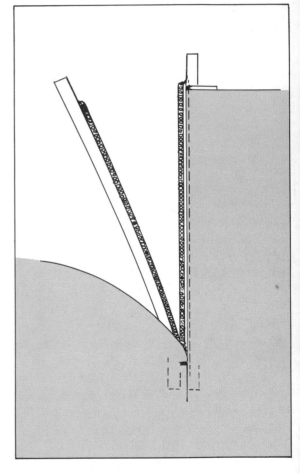

Lock threads by changing the stitch length to 0 and sewing several stitches in place. This method doesn't create bulk or puckers like backstitching .

4. Press LEFT front extension under 3/4". On RIGHT front, press extension under 1-1/2".

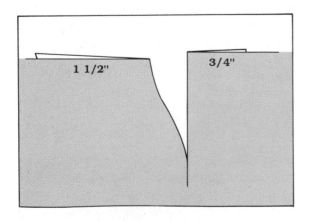

1 1/2"   3/4"

6. Lap RIGHT front extension to left side so center front lines meet. Pin in place. Topstitch beginning at bottom of zipper opening and curve stitching line at bottom.

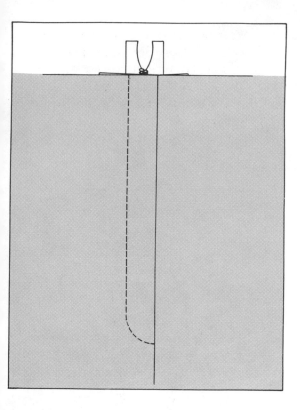

B. Clip to seam allowances before and after double stitching. Trim double stitched seam to 3/8" and zigzag raw edges together.

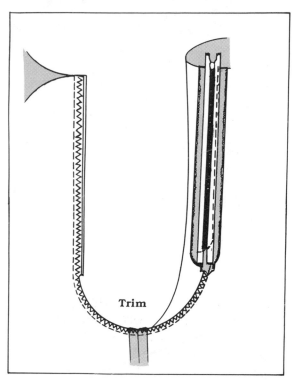

Trim

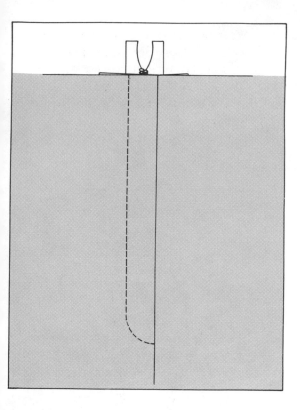 **Mark the stitching line for your fly front using a washable marking pen. Use a "Fly Front Zipper Guide" for accurate marking.**

Always sew zippers from bottom to top. Sewing from the waistline to the bottom may create a dimple at the bottom of the zipper.

7. Open zipper and bar tack across teeth close to fabric's cut edge. Cut off excess zipper table above bar tack.
   After completing the zipper, reinforce and trim the crotch seam:
   A. Stitch 1/4" from stitching line in curved area.

Fitting Notes

CHAPTER 5

CHECK YOUR FIT AND FINISH YOUR SLACKS

Getting Ready To Fit

For best results, find someone to help fit your slacks. Place 1/2" wide lingerie elastic around your waist and pin ends together. Put on your slacks and pin the cut edge to the lingerie elastic.

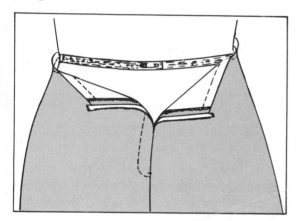

Know Your Wrinkles

Wrinkles are hints about fitting problems, so it's important to understand different types of wrinkles. Most references list three types of wrinkles: horizontal, vertical, and bias. But, there are actually six kinds: HORIZONTAL wrinkles that either PULL or FOLD, VERTICAL wrinkles that either PULL or FOLD, or BIAS wrinkles that either PULL or FOLD.

Horizontal Fold Wrinkles = too much length.

Vertical Fold Wrinkles = to much width.

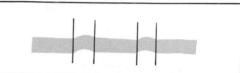

Bias Fold Wrinkle (a combination of Vertical and Horizontal) = too much length and width.

Any wrinkle that "pulls" is telling you that there is not enough fabric.

Horizontal Pull Wrinkles = not enough width.

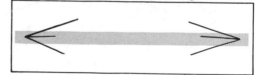

Vertical Pull Wrinkles = not enough width.

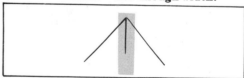

Bias Pull Wrinkles

(a combination of Vertical and Horizontal) = not enough length and width.

***Use these wrinkle character-
istics when working on any
fitting project.***

Swayback

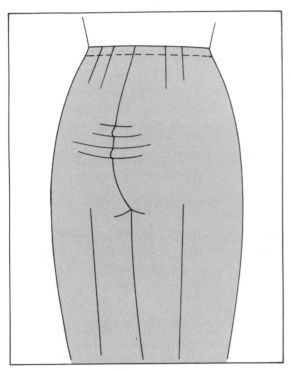

HORIZONTAL FOLDS at center back
are common, indicating a slight
sway. To remove extra length at
center back:

1. Remove pins at back waistline.
   Smooth up extra fabric. Repin to
   elastic.
2. Using a washable marking pen,
   mark the new waistline cutting
   line, following the top of the elastic.
3. Re-cut your fabric accurately by
   folding slacks at center back seam.
   Match center back cutting line at
   new waistline. (Your pattern will be
   at an angle.)

4. Trim excess fabric at back waistline. Trim the same amount from
   your pattern.

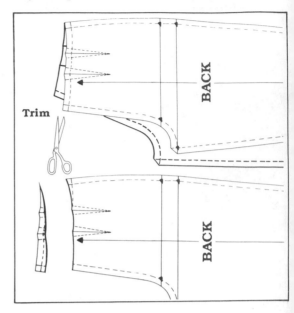

Seat Wrinkles

A curvy or rounded seat may cause
HORIZONTAL PULL wrinkles to
radiate out directly below the seat.
Eliminate these wrinkles by creating
a deeper curve at the back crotch.

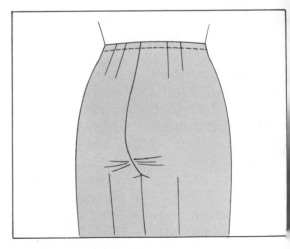

1. With a French curve, hollow out the back curve. Sew a deeper curve. Trim out excess seam allowances.
2. If wrinkles persist, follow steps for altering crotch wrinkles.

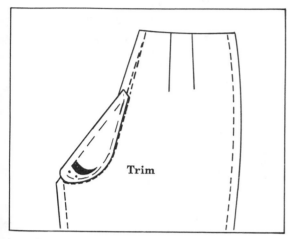

Crotch Wrinkles

Probably the most common wrinkles in slacks are HORIZONTAL FOLDS under the seat. This can be confusing. This wrinkle indicates **the inseam length is too long and the crotch length is too short.** (It doesn't mean the crotch is too long!)

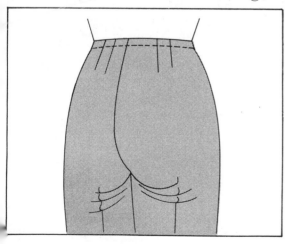

Remove these wrinkles easily on your new slacks and on slacks hanging in your closet:

1. Turn slacks wrongside out and stitch a deeper crotch seam. Sew a 1/2" deeper seam where the crotch curves, both on the front and the back.
2. Trim excess seam allowances.
3. Try your slacks on again. If you still see a wrinkle, repeat steps 1 & 2 with a 1/4" deeper seam allowance.

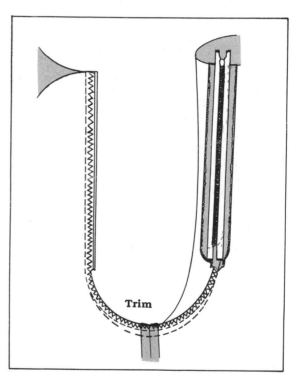

Fullness in Thigh

VERTICAL FOLDS in the thigh aren't too common, but they are easy to correct.

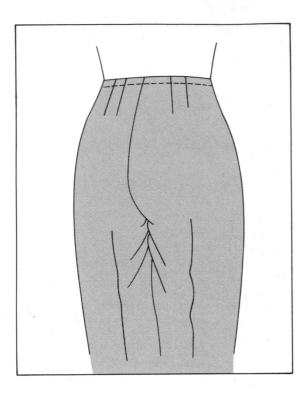

1. Release crotch seam where inseams meet.

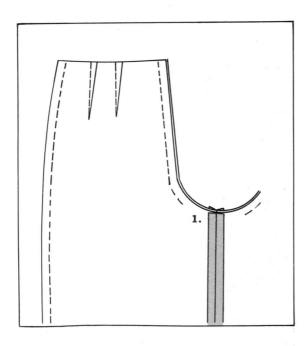

2. Fold slacks along inner seam. Place a pin 1/2-1" from inner seam sewing line.
3. Place pattern on slacks, matching pattern's cutting line to fabric's *sewing line.*
4. Place a pin at pattern's knee and PIVOT pattern to meet the pin at crotch. With marking pen, draw the new sewing line.

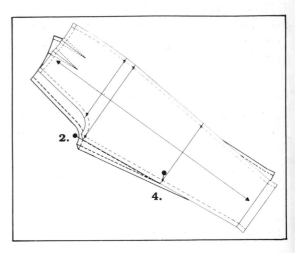

5. Stitch along new sewing line. Trim away excess fabric, leaving 5/8" seam allowance.

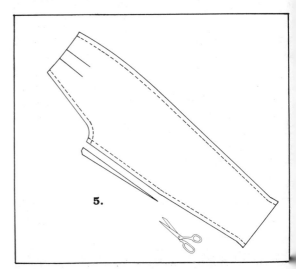

6. Try on slacks. If the crotch seems too short, sew a deeper crotch seam as explained in section on Crotch Wrinkles.

Front Crease Hangs Inward

In Alteration Unit 2, you altered for a High Hip. If your measurement was shorter than the pattern, you were asked to wait until this fitting step to shorten the side length.

If the side length is too long, the center front crease will bow inward. This may occur on one or both slacks legs.

1. Unpin slacks from elastic at side seam and smooth the fabric up until the center front crease hangs straight. Repin elastic. Mark new waist cutting line following the top of the elastic with a washable marking pen.

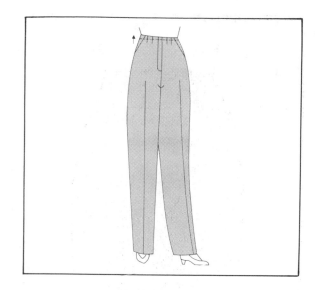

2. If both creases hang toward the center, fold slacks at center front and place pattern on fabric. Match pattern and fabric at *original* center front line. At the side seam, meet the pattern's waistline cutting line with *new* marking.

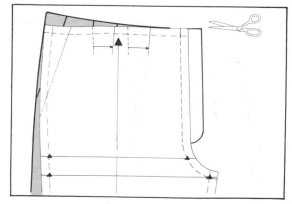

3. Trim excess fabric at waistline. Make same adjustment on pattern. Repeat Steps 2 and 3 on back of slacks.

Note: If only one crease bows inward, trim only that side of your slacks.

Front Crease Hangs Outward

If your measurements and alterations in Unit 2 were accurate, this should not occur. But if one hip is higher than the other, it may now become noticeable.

1. Release pins at side waistline until the front crease hangs straight. Repin.
2. When attaching waistband, sew a smaller seam allowance at the slacks sides. Make this change on the pattern as instructed in Alteration Unit 2.

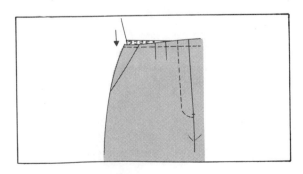

Bias Wrinkles in Thigh

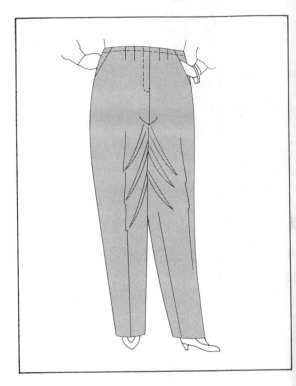

When walking, if bias wrinkles pull from the thigh area to the knee, it's an indication that the thigh is too narrow and the crotch length is too short. Sometimes these wrinkles cannot be totally eliminated after the slacks have been sewn since the seam allowances can be released only 3/8" per side. Here's how to lessen the wrinkle:

1. Turn the slacks inside out. Release the stitches at the crotch seam.
2. Sew a 1/4" seam allowance in the inseam, starting at the knee to the thigh. Sew a 1/4" seam allowance along the outside seam, starting at the knee and ending at the hipline.

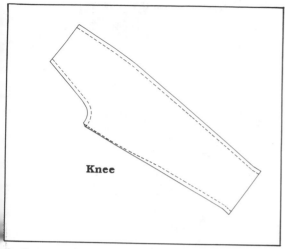

Knee

3. Sew a deeper crotch seam in the slacks front.
4. Trim off the extra seam allowance in the crotch seam.

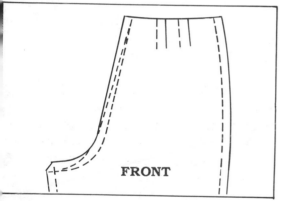

FRONT

5. Before making another pair of slacks, check the thigh measurement and the crotch length.

A Note About Wrinkles

Now that you've found the wrinkles in your slacks and corrected them, be sure to make the same changes on your pattern. Then when you make the next pair, this fitting step will be eliminated.

Finishing the Waistband

The waistband in this pattern comes in three pieces — two front pieces cut on grain and a contoured back piece cut on the bias. Custom or European made slacks ease in this slightly smaller back waistband to curve around the contour of the back. As a result, the waistband fits smoothly and hugs the body.

1. Cut 2 of each of the front waistbands and 2 of the back waistband. Interface with fusible interfacing that has the seam allowances trimmed off.

For a handy interfacing pattern, put wax paper over the waistband lengths. Place the edge of your tape measure against the cut edge of fabric. Trace along the other side of the tape with a pencil. The tape measure accurately produces a 5/8" seam.

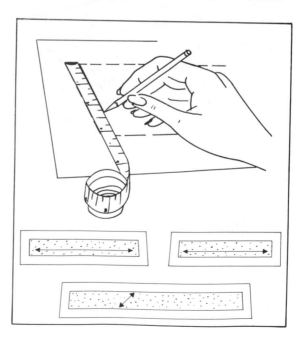

Cut interfacing on same grain as fashion fabric; fuse to the wrong side of the fabric.

2. Sew waistbands together at side seams. You will have two waistbands - an outer and inner band.

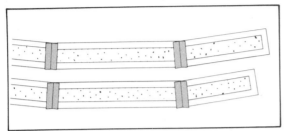

3. With rightsides together, sew your waistbands together along the upper edge. Grade and understitch.

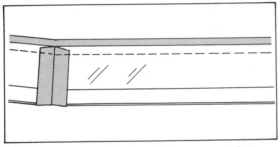

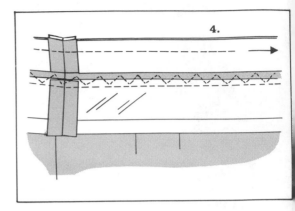

Understitch with a multiple zigzag or the widest zigzag on your machine. This additional thread will give the top of your waistband greater support.

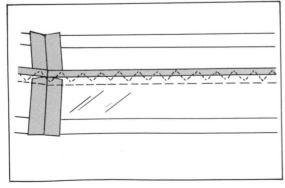

4. With right side of waistband meeting right side of slacks, stitch a 5/8" seam.

This back waistband is designed to be 1/2" smaller than the garment for a smoother fit. Ease together automatically; place the larger piece next to the feed dogs and stitch.

5. Grade seam allowances and press up.

6. Trim 3/8" off inner waistline seam. Finish this raw edge with Seams Great®, a zigzag stitch or a serged/overlock stitch.

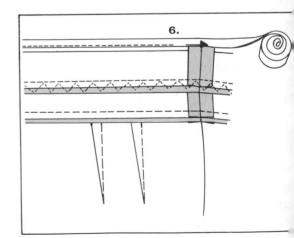

7. Place center fronts of waistband with right sides together. Sew center front seams. Trim bulk and turn right sides out.

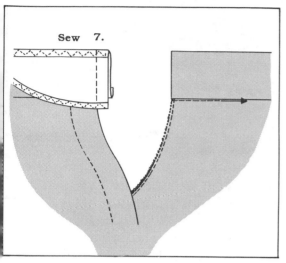

Sew 7.

8. Finish waistband and attach inner waistband by "stitching in the ditch." This term refers to stitching from the right side in the seam "ditch" catching only the under fabric.

9. Sew on a hook and eye or button and buttonholes. Add threadloops or belt carriers if you like.

Elasticized Waistband

Any slacks pattern can easily be changed to an elasticized style. This style is best suited for those figures whose waist and hip measurements *differ by 10" or less.*

To change your "Pivot-Slide Slacks Pattern" to an elasticized waistband:

1. On front pattern, fold back the fly extension. If making slacks with side pockets, pin pocket pattern piece to front piece.

2. Extend width at hip up to waistline on center front and side seams using a ruler. Omit darts or pleats. Repeat on back.

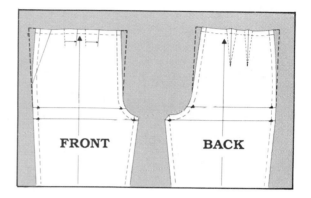

FRONT   BACK

3. Sew slacks as detailed.

4. Cut waistband pattern 3-1/2" wide X the length needed to fit the new waistline plus 1-1/4" for the seam allowance.

5. Right sides together, sew waistband into a circle. Leave an opening in this seam for inserting the elastic. (Lockstitch or back stitch on either side of this opening for reinforcement.)

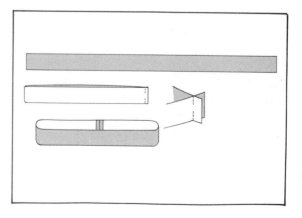

6. Press open the seam. With *wrong* sides of waistband together, pin raw edges of waistband to raw edges of waistline. Sew all three layers together.

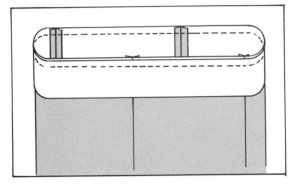

7. Trim seam allowances to 3/8" and zigzag or serge raw edges together. Press seam allowances down toward slacks.

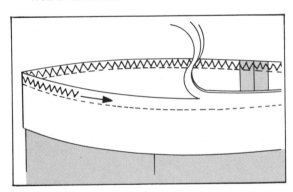

8. Cut 1" non-roll elastic to a comfortable length.

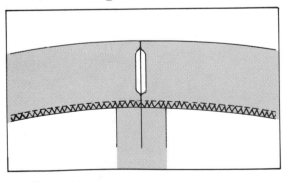

9. Thread elastic through the opening in your waistband. Try on slacks and adjust for comfort.

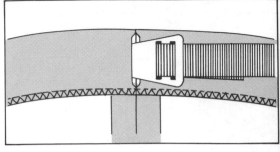

10. Remove garment.
11. Stitch ends of elastic securely. Cut off excess.
12. Distribute fullness evenly.
13. Secure elastic by stitching through all layers in the groove of each seam.

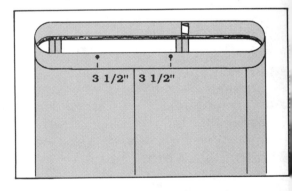

3 1/2"   3 1/2"

For a more fitted look, keep elastic flat at the center front. Follow steps 1-10. Before sewing elastic together, measure 3-1/2" on each side of center front. Sew elastic to waistband with a row of straight stitches between 3-1/2" marks. Keep the elastic flat while stitching. Sew elastic ends together. Follow steps 12 and 13.

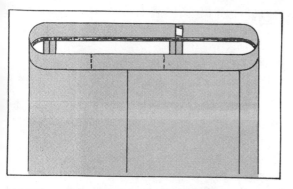

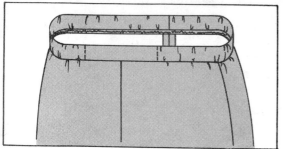

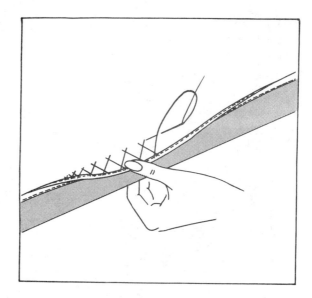

Hem Legs

This pattern allows a 1-1/4" hem allowance. Press up the hem and trim seam allowances to 1/4-3/8". Zigzag, serge, or clean finish raw edges with Seams Great®. Blind hem with your machine or catch stitch the hem by hand. (See illustration.)

Congratulations! Your slacks are now complete! *Use your new personalized pattern and the contemporary sewing techniques in this book, to stitch up several more pairs of slacks that will enhance your wardrobe.*

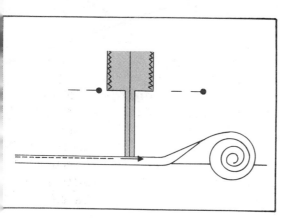

Other Books By Nancy Zieman

The Busy Woman's Fitting Book
By Nancy Zieman with Robbie Fanning

The busier we are, the more simplified we need to make some of our routine tasks. As sewers, we need to simplify the routine task of fitting patterns. To ease the fitting dilemma, Nancy and Robbie have broken down the common problems of fitting blouses, tops, dresses, and blazers (slacks not included) into a series of "Fitting Challenges and Solutions." Each fitting challenge is easily corrected by using Pivot and Slide alteration techniques. Each chapter is written with step-by-step directions and concentrates on a particular area of the figure. 118 pages. $9.95

The Busy Woman's Sewing Book
By Nancy Zieman with Robbie Fanning

Nancy Zieman shows you the secrets of fast sewing— the key to saving time is to get organized and to use contemporary sewing techniques. In this book you see how to plan a season's wardrobe by perfecting one semi-lined jacket, blouse, casual top, skirt, and slacks pattern. With this plan you can sew faster than you could shop. In the process you will learn modern sewing techniques like how to use fusible interfacings and sew with sergers, as well as many time-saving sewing techniques. 118 pages. $9.95

Order these books through the Nancy's Notions Sewing Catalog — your source for sewing books, notions, videos, and fabrics. To receive your FREE Catalog, send your name and address to:

Nancy's Notions, Ltd.
P.O. Box 683—Dept. SB
Beaver Dam, WI   53916-0683

Or, Call Direct Order Line:
414-887-0690

Index